1 PIANO, 4 HANDS

PIANO DUET PLAY-ALONG

VOLUME 43

A MERRY LITTLE CHRISTMAS

ISBN 978-1-4768-1283-0

HAL•LEONARD®
CORPORATION

7777 W. BLUEMOUND RD. P.O. BOX 13819 MILWAUKEE, WI 53213

Visit Hal Leonard Online at
www.halleonard.com

CONTENTS

ALL I WANT FOR CHRISTMAS IS
MY TWO FRONT TEETH

SECONDO

Words and Music by
DON GARDNER

ALL I WANT FOR CHRISTMAS IS
MY TWO FRONT TEETH

PRIMO

Words and Music by
DON GARDNER

SECONDO

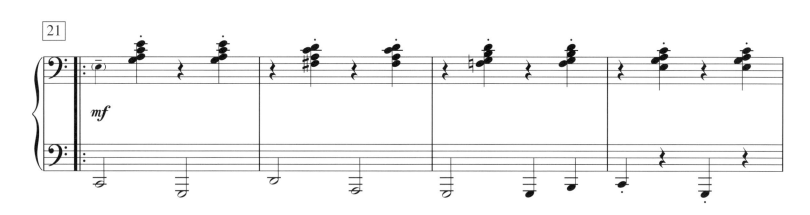

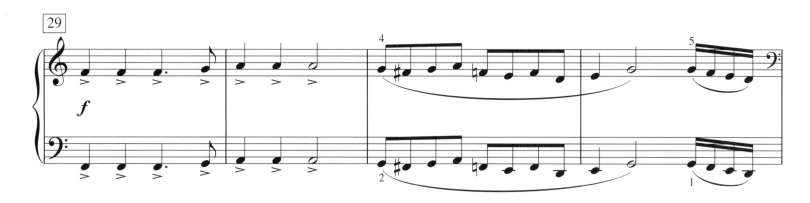

PRIMO

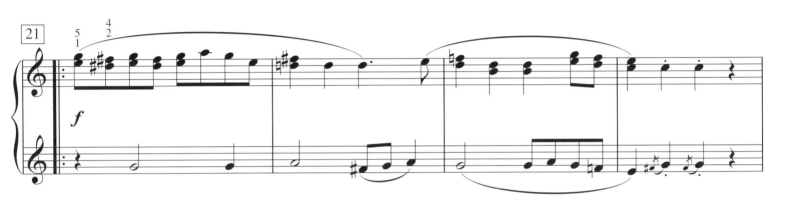

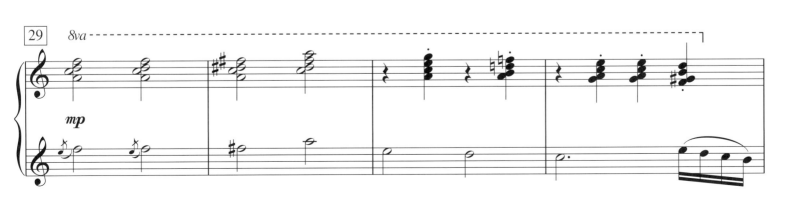

SECONDO

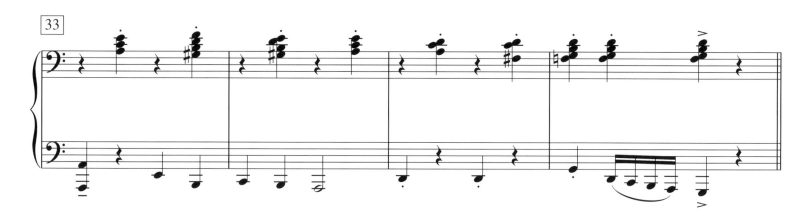

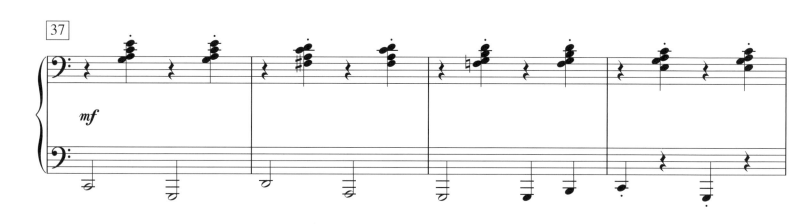

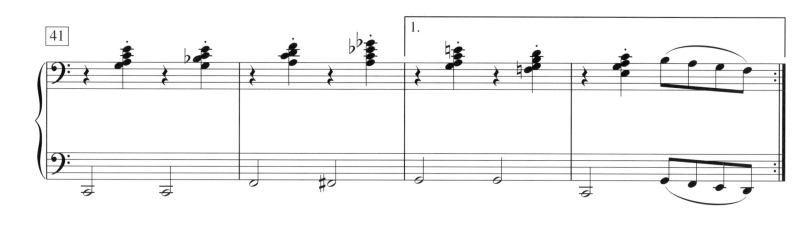

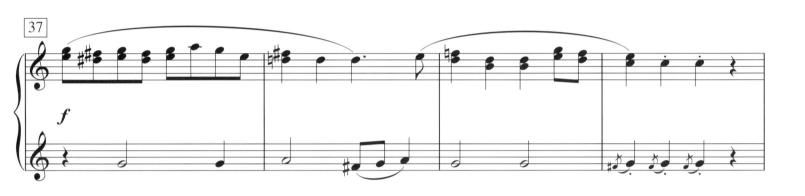

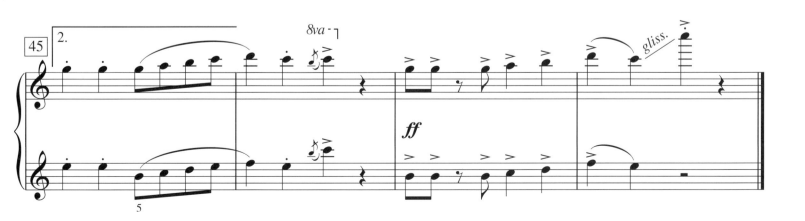

BELIEVE
from Warner Bros. Pictures' THE POLAR EXPRESS

SECONDO

Words and Music by GLEN BALLARD
and ALAN SILVESTRI

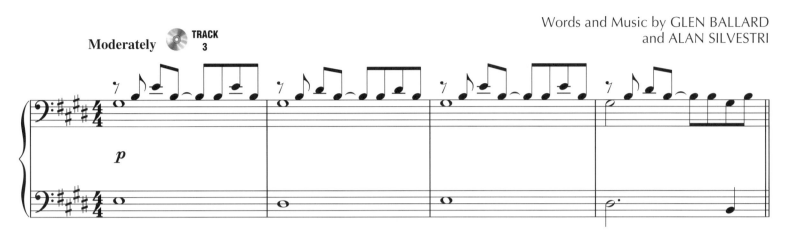

BELIEVE
from Warner Bros. Pictures' THE POLAR EXPRESS

PRIMO

Words and Music by GLEN BALLARD
and ALAN SILVESTRI

SECONDO

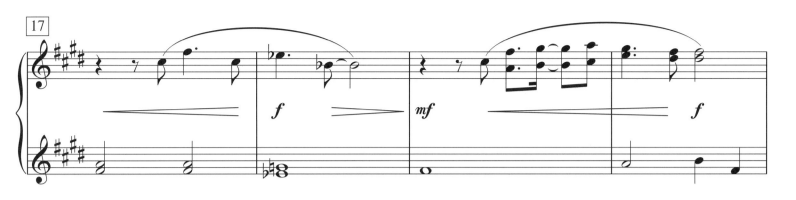

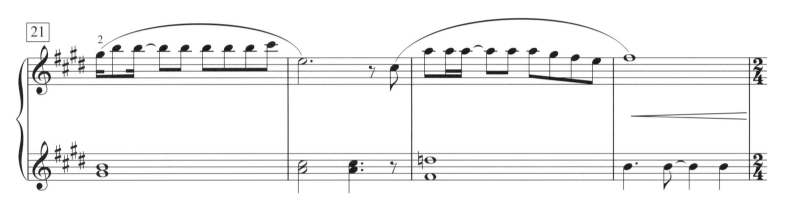

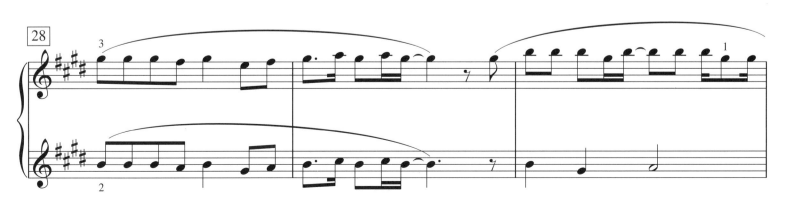

SECONDO

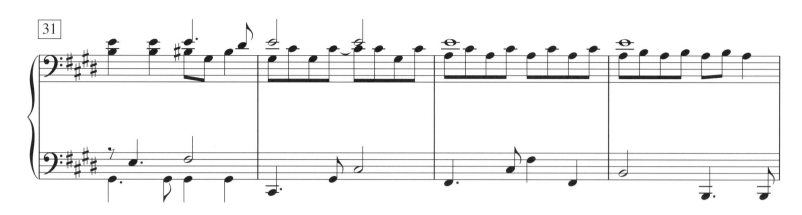

PRIMO

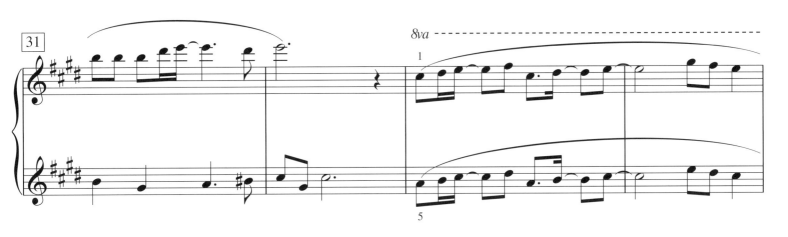

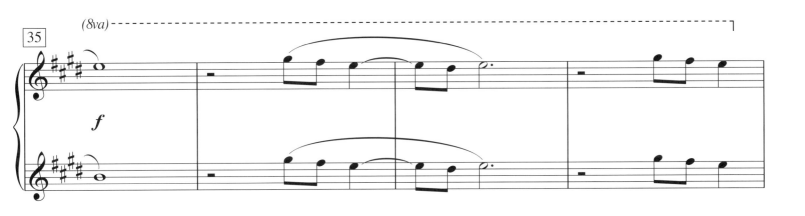

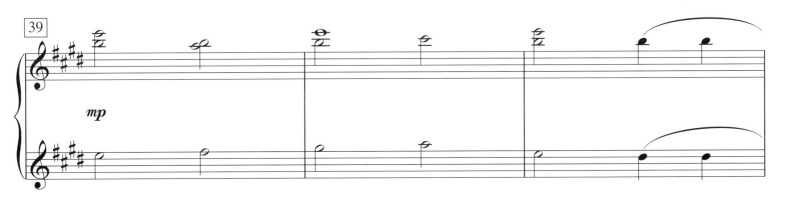

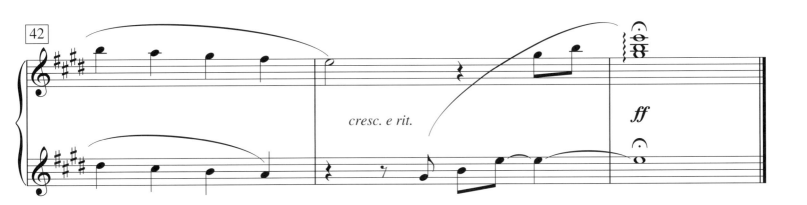

GROWN-UP CHRISTMAS LIST

SECONDO

Words and Music by DAVID FOSTER
and LINDA THOMPSON-JENNER

GROWN-UP CHRISTMAS LIST

PRIMO

Words and Music by DAVID FOSTER
and LINDA THOMPSON-JENNER

SECONDO

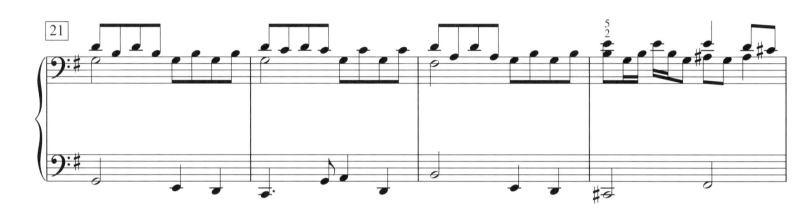

PRIMO

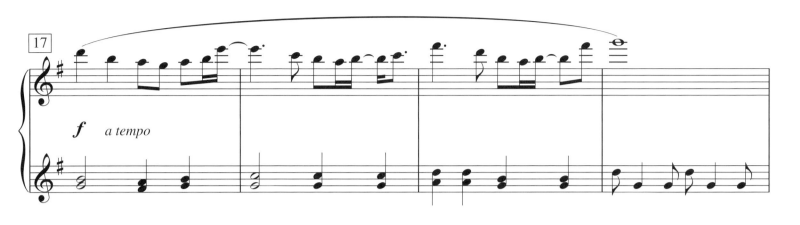

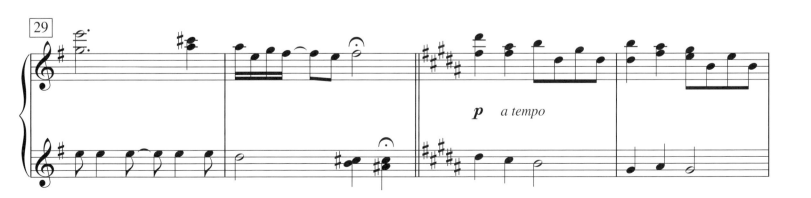

SECONDO

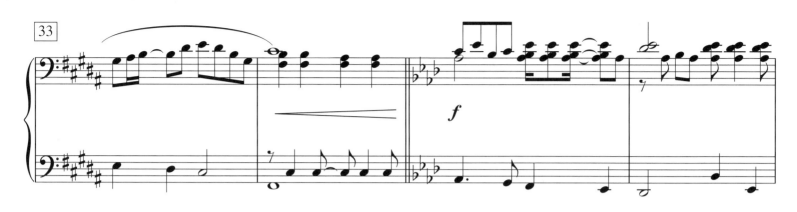

PRIMO

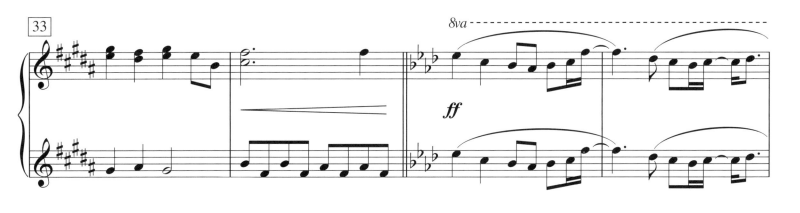

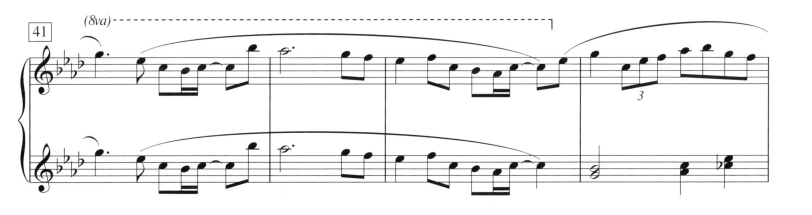

HAVE YOURSELF A MERRY LITTLE CHRISTMAS

from MEET ME IN ST. LOUIS

SECONDO

Words and Music by HUGH MARTIN
and RALPH BLANE

HAVE YOURSELF A MERRY LITTLE CHRISTMAS

from MEET ME IN ST. LOUIS

PRIMO

Words and Music by HUGH MARTIN
and RALPH BLANE

SECONDO

PRIMO

THE MOST WONDERFUL TIME OF THE YEAR

SECONDO

Words and Music by EDDIE POLA
and GEORGE WYLE

THE MOST WONDERFUL
TIME OF THE YEAR

PRIMO

Words and Music by EDDIE POLA
and GEORGE WYLE

PRIMO

SECONDO

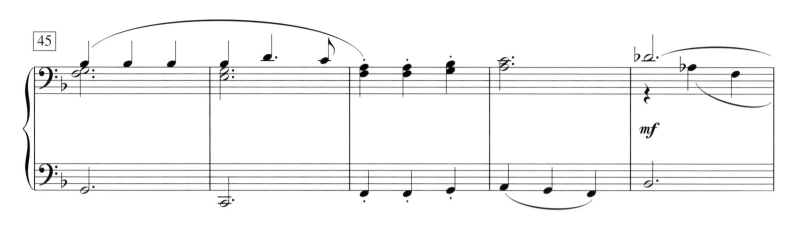

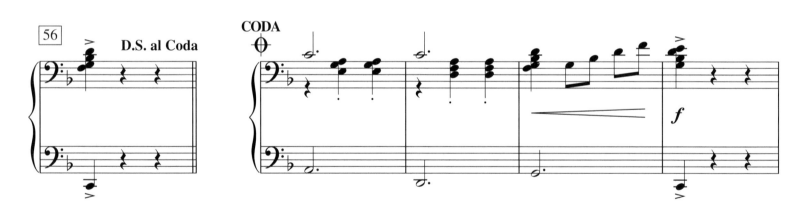

PRIMO

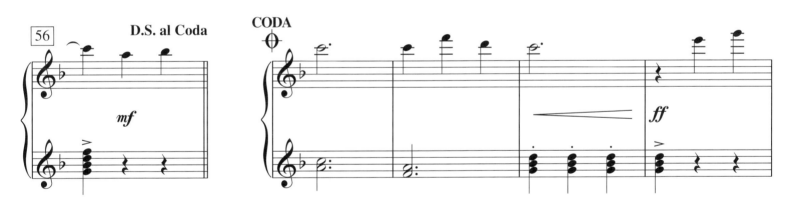

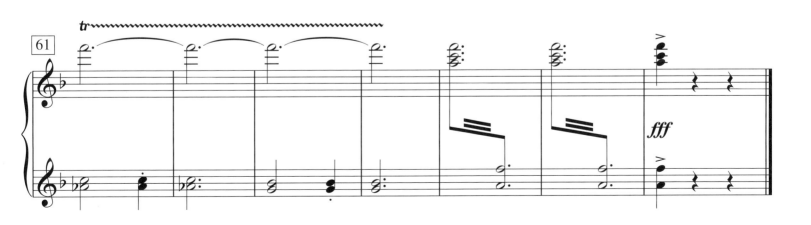

SLEIGH RIDE

SECONDO

Music by LEROY ANDERSON
Words by MITCHELL PARISH

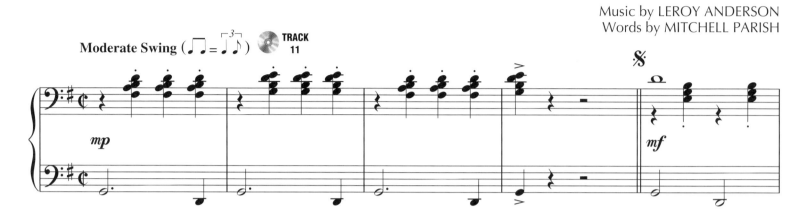

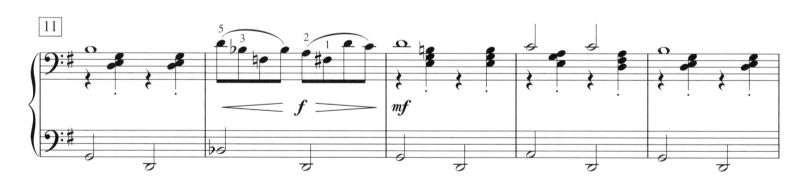

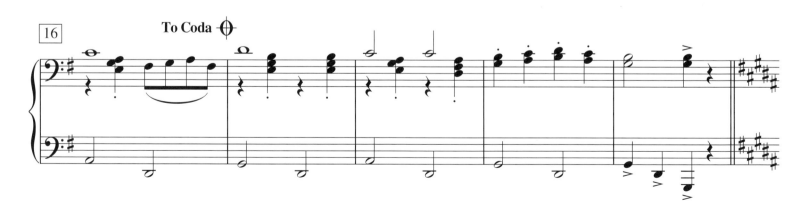

SLEIGH RIDE

PRIMO

Music by LEROY ANDERSON
Words by MITCHELL PARISH

SOMEWHERE IN MY MEMORY
from the Twentieth Century Fox Motion Picture HOME ALONE

SECONDO

Words by LESLIE BRICUSSE
Music by JOHN WILLIAMS

SOMEWHERE IN MY MEMORY
from the Twentieth Century Fox Motion Picture HOME ALONE

PRIMO

Words by LESLIE BRICUSSE
Music by JOHN WILLIAMS

SECONDO

WINTER WONDERLAND

SECONDO

Words by DICK SMITH
Music by FELIX BERNARD

WINTER WONDERLAND

PRIMO

Words by DICK SMITH
Music by FELIX BERNARD

SECONDO

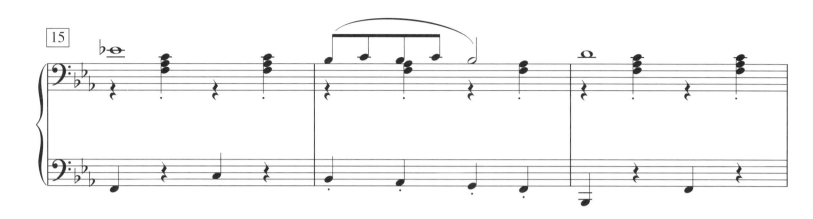

PRIMO

SECONDO

PRIMO

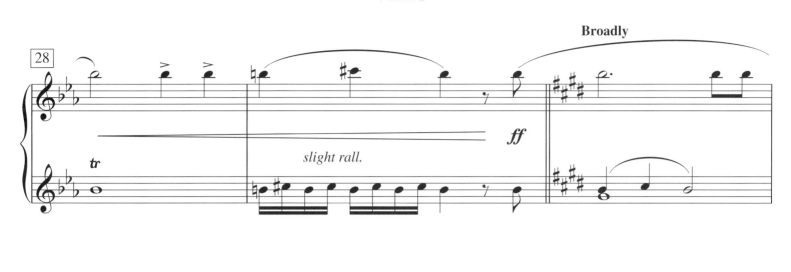

PIANO DUETS

The **Piano Duet Play-Along** series is an excellent source for 1 Piano, 4 Hand duets in every genre! It also gives you the flexibility to rehearse or perform piano duets anytime, anywhere! Play these delightful tunes with a partner, or use the accompanying CDs to play along with either the Secondo or Primo part on your own. The CD is enhanced so PC and Mac users can adjust the recording to any tempo without changing pitch.

1. Piano Favorites
00290546 Book/CD Pack $14.95

2. Movie Favorites
00290547 Book/CD Pack $14.95

3. Broadway for Two
00290548 Book/CD Pack $14.95

**4. The Music of
Andrew Lloyd Webber™**
00290549 Book/CD Pack $14.95

5. Disney Favorites
00290550 Book/CD Pack $14.95

6. Disney Songs
00290551 Book/CD Pack $14.95

7. Classical Music
00290552 Book/CD Pack $14.95

8. Christmas Classics
00290554 Book/CD Pack $14.95

9. Hymns
00290556 Book/CD Pack $14.95

10. The Sound of Music
00290557 Book/CD Pack $17.99

11. Disney Early Favorites
00290558 Book/CD Pack $16.95

12. Disney Movie Songs
00290559 Book/CD Pack $16.95

13. Movie Hits
00290560 Book/CD Pack $14.95

14. Les Misérables
00290561 Book/CD Pack $16.95

**15. God Bless America® & Other
Songs for a Better Nation**
00290562 Book/CD Pack $14.99

16. Disney Classics
00290563 Book/CD Pack $16.95

17. High School Musical
00290564 Book/CD Pack $16.95

18. High School Musical 2
00290565 Book/CD Pack $16.99

19. Pirates of the Caribbean
00290566 Book/CD Pack $16.95

20. Wicked
00290567 Book/CD Pack $16.99

21. Peanuts®
00290568 Book/CD Pack $16.99

22. Rodgers & Hammerstein
00290569 Book/CD Pack $14.99

23. Cole Porter
00290570 Book/CD Pack $14.99

24. Christmas Carols
00290571 Book/CD Pack $14.95

25. Wedding Songs
00290572 Book/CD Pack $14.99

26. Love Songs
00290573 Book/CD Pack $14.99

27. Romantic Favorites
00290574 Book/CD Pack $14.99

28. Classical for Two
00290575 Book/CD Pack $14.99

29. Broadway Classics
00290576 Book/CD Pack $14.99

30. Jazz Standards
00290577 Book/CD Pack $14.99

31. Pride and Prejudice
00290578 Book/CD Pack $14.99

32. Sondheim for Two
00290579 Book/CD Pack $16.99

33. Twilight
00290580 Book/CD Pack $14.99

34. Hannah Montana
00290581 Book/CD Pack $16.99

35. High School Musical 3
00290582 Book/CD Pack $16.99

36. Holiday Favorites
00290583 Book/CD Pack $14.99

37. Christmas for Two
00290584 Book/CD Pack $14.99

38. Lennon & McCartney Favorites
00290585 Book/CD Pack $14.99

39. Lennon & McCartney Hits
00290586 Book/CD Pack $14.99

40. Classical Themes
00290588 Book/CD Pack $14.99

41. The Phantom of the Opera
00290589 Book/CD Pack $16.99

42. Glee
00290590 Book/CD Pack $16.99

FOR MORE INFORMATION, SEE YOUR LOCAL MUSIC DEALER,
OR WRITE TO:

**HAL•LEONARD®
CORPORATION**
7777 W. BLUEMOUND RD. P.O. BOX 13819 MILWAUKEE, WI 53213

Visit Hal Leonard Online at **www.halleonard.com**

Disney characters and artwork are © Disney Enterprises, Inc.

0810